Gary just didn't know the rules

by Holly-ann Martin

Gary just didn't know the rules
by Holly-ann Martin

Published March 2018
by Safe 4 Kids (Aust) Pty Ltd
www.safe4kids.com.au
PO Box 367
Armadale WA 6992
Australia

Illustrations by Marilyn Fahie
Cover designed by Steve Horton

Printed by CreateSpace,
an Amazon.com Company

A catalogue record for this book is available from the National Library of Australia

ISBN-13: 978-0-6482877-2-8 (paperback)

I dedicate this book to my wonderful husband Roger, without whose love and support I couldn't do what I do.

Together we can help make the world a safer place for children to grow up in.

Note to Parents, Carers and Teachers

I have written this book to help parents, carers and teachers address the issue of child-to-child sexual abuse. Increasingly I have been contacted by childcare centres and primary schools that have experienced cases of child-to-child sexual abuse and are not sure how to educate parents, carers, their staff and children, to try and prevent any further instances occurring. It is a confronting subject, but I hope this book will provide you and your children with the necessary skills to help combat this problem.

This book is designed for adults to read to children to educate them about this subject in a safe non-threatening manner. It is important to protect the innocence of children and not provide them with too much information or cause trauma. In order to achieve this, I have developed five "private rules". These rules provide children with clear and concise guidelines about any inappropriate touching, viewing pornography, taking pictures of their private body parts or other people taking pictures of their private body parts. In this book I refer to pornography as "private pictures" or "private movies". This helps reinforce the concept of public and private with the children.

These five private rules are designed to help keep children safe from sexual abuse at home, at school, in fact anywhere they go. They are designed to empower children to help keep themselves safe.

In this story, an "incident" occurs in the boys' toilet, involving Gary. I have deliberately not detailed the incident to protect the innocence of children and to try and avoid any additional trauma to children who may have experienced sexual abuse. On pages 32-33 there are discussion questions that give children the opportunity to brainstorm what may have happened in the boys' toilet. This will give parents and educators the chance to see if children have understood the key concepts and to provide further explanation appropriate to the children's comprehension level.

It is advisable that you read this book first, including the Information for Parents, Carers and Teachers section, before reading it to your children; to familiarise yourself with the content and prepare for any discussions that may arise. If you are not familiar with the core concepts of Protective Education included in this story, please refer to the Additional Information section on pages 33-36 for further details.

I hope you and your children enjoy this book.

Holly-ann Martin

Gary just didn't know the rules is the fourth in a series of educational children's books on child-abuse-prevention education.

The first book in this series, *Matilda learns a valuable lesson*, looks at unwanted touching (non-sexual) and teaches children if they feel unsafe they need to seek help from an adult they trust. If one adult doesn't listen, then they need to persist and tell another adult they trust and to keep telling until an adult helps them, and they feel safe again.

The second book in this series, *Hayden-Reece learns a valuable lesson that Private means 'Just for you'* teaches children the correct anatomical names for their private body parts and that no one should see or touch their private body parts without their consent. The book follows a logical progression and discusses public and private rooms, body functions, behaviours, language and clothing, and culminates in private body parts. It is essential children know the correct anatomical names for their private body parts as it can be a protective factor in deterring a potential perpetrator.

The third book in this series, *Hayden-Reece Learns What To Do if Children See Private Pictures or Private Movies*, follows on from the first Hayden-Reece story. It revises the concept of public and private and then leads into the discussion on private pictures and private movies (pornography). This book provides both children and adults with strategies suggesting what to do if children view pornography either by accident, intentionally or are shown pornography by an adult or another child.

Miss Martin was deep in discussion with her class. They were discussing what 'Human Rights' are.
Suddenly there was a knock at the door and Mrs Langley, the principal, stepped into the room, followed by a young boy.
"Good morning, Miss Martin," she said.

"You have a new student. His name is Gary and he will be joining your class."

Miss Martin smiled.

"Welcome, Gary. Would you like to sit here on the floor next to Elliot, and we'll find you a desk when we have finished our lesson."

Mrs Langley left and Miss Martin continued her lesson.

"Gary, our lesson is on something called Protective Education which is about kids learning to keep themselves safe. In Protective Education we have two life rules. Today we are looking at the first life rule: "We all have the right to feel safe all of the time", and we are talking about the United Nations Human Rights of the Child, which are designed to help keep children safe. Can anyone explain to Gary what Human Rights are?"

Lots of hands went up.

"Yes, Lauren, what are Human Rights?"

"Human Rights are a big long list of things our government has agreed to, that every child in Australia should have. They don't have to be earned – you are born with them."

"Excellent, Lauren! Can anyone give me an example of a Human Right?"

"The right to have food when you are hungry," answered Mary. "Some children in other countries don't have enough food to eat."

"The right to have an education," said Jeremy. "In some countries girls can't go to school and get an education; only boys go to school."

"That's not fair," said Hayden-Reece.

"The right to play and not have to work like a grown-up," declared Brendon. "I watched a documentary where even very young children had to go to work at a rubbish dump and collect bits of plastic. They didn't even have shoes or gloves."

"I'm so glad I don't
live there,"
said Hayden-Reece.
The bell went and
Miss Martin let the children
go out to play.
Hayden-Reece asked
Gary to join in a
game of four square.
Gary seemed
to settle well into
Miss Martin's class until
about a week later.

David came into class after recess. He seemed rather quiet and Miss Martin knew something was wrong. At lunchtime, after all the other children went out to play, David said, "Miss Martin, can I tell you something?"

"Of course, David. You know you can talk with me about anything."

"You always teach us that when we feel unsafe, when we get our Early Warning Signs, we should tell someone on our Safety Team – but it's not easy," said David.

"Take your time." Miss Martin spoke very gently.

David went on to tell Miss Martin about something private that happened in the boys' toilet at recess time, involving Gary, which gave him his Early Warning Signs.

"I'm so glad you told me, David. I believe you; it wasn't your fault and I will deal with it. Gary is new to our school and he just doesn't know the Public and Private rules."

David felt much better after telling Miss Martin what had happened and knew she would do something about it.

David's Early Warning Signs went away and he went off to lunch, feeling much safer.

After lunch Miss Martin asked all the children to come and sit on the floor in front of her.

"This afternoon we are going to revise the Public and Private lesson I taught you. Who can tell me what 'private' means?"

All the children put up their hands, except for Gary.

"Yes, Lauren?"

"Private means just for you."

"Well done, Lauren."

"Who can tell me the names of the three private rooms in your home?"

Hayden-Reece's hand shot up.

Miss Martin said, "Yes, Hayden-Reece?"

"Bedrooms, bathrooms and toilets are private rooms and what makes them private is when you shut the door. You mustn't play in the toilets – you just go in, go to the toilet, wash your hands and come out."

Hayden-Reece looked very pleased with himself. He was thinking back to the time he made the mistake of looking over the wall at Lauren in the girls' toilet, before he knew the Rules. Miss Martin gave him a knowing wink and said, "Exactly right."

“What are the names of our private body parts?” asked Miss Martin.

Elliot named all the boys’ private body parts – mouth, bottom, penis and testicles. Gary laughed, but Miss Martin didn’t tell him off.

Karen named all the girls' private body parts – mouth, breasts, bottom, vulva and vagina.

"Well done, everyone. You have remembered everything I've taught you." Miss Martin beamed at the children. "Now we are going to learn something new. I'm going to teach you the 'five private rules'. If you follow these rules they will help keep you safe at home, at school, in fact anywhere you go. If anyone breaks these five private rules and you get your Early Warning Signs and feel unsafe, you need to tell someone on your Safety Team. Who can tell me what a Safety Team is?" Miss Martin waited.

Cameron was the first to put his hand up.

"Yes, Cameron?"

"A Safety Team is five trusted adults you can talk to about anything. They need to know what has happened so they can help you feel safe again."

"Excellent, Cameron!" Miss Martin smiled. "Now let's get started on the five private rules.

"Rule number one. No-one, not other children, teenagers or adults and even teenagers or adults in your family, should touch your private body parts, except for medical reasons or to help keep you clean, and then they should ask you for your permission to do so. If someone does touch your private parts, it's not your fault – they are breaking the law."

Miss Martin paused and looked around.

"Who can tell me what breaking the law means?"

Karen explained, “Laws are rules that the government makes, that everyone in the country must obey; the police make sure everyone follows these laws to help keep us all safe. Breaking the law means not obeying these rules.”

“Well done, Karen, great answer,” said Miss Martin.

“Rule number two. You are not allowed to touch ANYONE else’s private body parts. Sometimes children might think it’s a game or funny to touch others’ private parts, but it is actually against the law.

“Rule number three. No-one should show you private pictures or private movies. Remember, we learnt what to do if you see private pictures or private movies. If you see pictures like that by accident, you say, ‘That’s private,’ and turn away; then go and tell an adult on your Safety Team. But if anyone – another child, teenager or grown-up; even a member of your family – shows you these kinds of pictures or movies, that is against the law. If you come across private pictures or private movies, you must not show other children because that would also be against the law.

"Rule number four. No-one is allowed to take private pictures of you. Sometimes adults make mistakes and might take pictures of children playing in the bath or naked under a sprinkler, because they think it's cute, but this is NOT OKAY; it is against the law.

"Rule number five. You are not allowed to take private pictures of yourself. Sometimes teenagers don't know these rules and make mistakes by taking pictures of their private body parts.

"If you have older brothers or sisters doing this you might think it's fun and copy them, but it is against the law too. Remember private means 'just for you'.

"So, those are the the five private rules to help keep you safe. If anyone breaks these rules and you get your Early Warning Signs and feel unsafe, you need to tell someone on your Safety Team, and keep telling until someone listens to you."

Gary had been listening very carefully during the lesson and looked thoughtful as all the children left the classroom that afternoon. He stayed behind and spoke to Miss Martin. "Miss Martin, can I tell you something?"

"Of course you can, Gary, you can tell me anything." Gary told Miss Martin about something that had been worrying him for a long time.

"I'm glad you told me, Gary. I believe you and that wasn't your fault. You were very brave to tell me about it and I'm going to do what I can to help keep you safe."

Gary felt so much better after talking with Miss Martin and he was very glad he had come to this new school.

Information for Parents, Carers and Teachers

It is important that parents, carers and teachers are able to distinguish between normal sexual curiosity and problem sexual behaviour that may indicate a child has been abused and is re-enacting what happened to them or what they may have seen, either in real life or in digital media. Children are naturally curious about their bodies and the bodies of others and will want to see if they are assembled in the same way. Sexual curiosity is normal and usually short-lived; it tends to be more visual than tactile. However, children who engage in problem sexual behaviours may use oral or digital penetration and use coercion and secrecy to keep from being discovered.

For more information regarding sexual behaviours in children and adolescents you might like to refer to: *TRAFFIC LIGHTS – sexual behaviours from birth to eighteen.*

https://nanangoss.eq.edu.au/Supportandresources/Formsanddocuments/Documents/traffic-lights.pdf

The following information is from a document titled "Children with problem sexual behaviours and their families: best interests case practice model: specialist practice resource" by Jari Evertsz and Robyn Miller, published in 2012, and is being shared with permission from the Department of Health and Human Services Victoria.

PRACTICAL RESPONSES TO CHILDREN ENGAGED IN PROBLEM SEXUAL BEHAVIOURS

Responding immediately to problem sexual behaviours engaged in by children is crucial. As adults we have individual values and attitudes about sexual behaviour which may result in either minimising or over-reacting to the observed behaviours. The initial response to the behaviour by people around the child is important and can significantly impact on the child's ability or willingness to address the behaviours.

When you or others observe problem sexual behaviours:

- Remain calm.
- Externalise the behaviour, i.e. separate and comment on the behaviour – do not demonise the child.
- Clearly and calmly ask the child to stop the behaviour.

- Separate the children and prioritise the safety and emotional wellbeing of the child who has been victimised. Reassure the victim child and provide comfort as required.
- Then engage separately and remain calm and non-punitive with the child who has enacted or initiated the problematic sexual behaviour. Be clear and firm that it is not okay, and note the child's explanation. Sometimes the child will be open and engage in conversation around the origins of the behaviour, e.g. 'Uncle Fred showed me this game and I was showing Terry'. It is crucial to remain low-key and conversational.
- Notice any unusual emotions in either of the children. Do they appear angry, agitated or upset? Make a note of this.
- Either child may become distressed and require nurture. If either child becomes angry and blames the other child, ensure that there is line-of-sight supervision and clear messages are given about boundaries and rules, particularly attending to any bullying or potential for retribution. Ensure safety and seek advice and expert assistance as soon as possible.
- Keep a record of the behaviour including the actions themselves, the context, date, times and frequency. (Note: this should be done discreetly and not used as a way of punishing children.)

After noticing worrying sexual behaviour, seek professional help.

Walking in on a seemingly abusive situation can be a shock for the adults involved. There are some common mistakes people make when they have witnessed/discovered sexual behaviours between children. Try not to:

- appear shocked
- react in such a way that will make the child feel embarrassed or ashamed
- ignore the behaviour
- automatically assume that sexual abuse has occurred – some sexual behaviour between children is normal

- use language that labels a child as a "pervert" or "sex offender"
- conduct a formal disclosure interview.

However, if the child is wanting to talk, remain attuned and engaged, letting them know that you are listening and it is okay to talk. Note down the child's disclosures as soon as possible – the details matter.

DISCUSSION QUESTIONS

Below are some questions you can ask children to see if they have understood the key concepts of this book. This will also give you the opportunity to provide further information if required, which is appropriate to the comprehension level of the children you are working with.

- Can you name any of the United Nations Human Rights of the Child from the story?
- Why did David want to talk to Miss Martin?
- Brainstorm with the children: What do you think the private thing that happened to David in the boys' toilet was? (It might have been Gary looking under the door, or over the wall. It might have been Gary showing private pictures or private movies. It might have been Gary trying to touch David's private body parts or having David touch Gary's private body parts.)
- What are the five private rules? (Reiterate what the five rules are)

RULE NUMBER ONE. No-one, not other children, teenagers or adults and even teenagers or adults in your family, should touch your private body parts, except for medical reasons or to help keep you clean, and then they should ask you for your permission to do so. If someone does touch your private parts, it's not your fault – they are breaking the law.

RULE NUMBER TWO. You are not allowed to touch ANYONE else's private body parts. Sometimes children might think it's a game or funny to touch others' private parts, but it is actually against the law.

RULE NUMBER THREE. No-one should show you private pictures or private movies. If you see pictures like that by accident, you say, "That's private," and turn away; then go and tell an adult on your Safety Team. But if anyone – another child, teenager or grown-up; even a member of your family – shows you these kinds of pictures or movies, that is against the law. If you come across private pictures or private movies, you must not show other children because that would also be against the law.

RULE NUMBER FOUR. No-one is allowed to take private pictures of you. Sometimes adults make mistakes and might take pictures of children playing in the bath or naked under a sprinkler, because they think it's cute, but this is not NOT OKAY; it is against the law.

RULE NUMBER FIVE. You are not allowed to take private pictures of yourself. Sometimes teenagers don't know these rules and make mistakes by taking pictures of their private body parts. If you have older brothers or sisters doing this you might think it's fun and copy them, but it is against the law too. Remember private means "Just for you".

If anyone breaks these rules and you get your Early Warning Signs and feel unsafe, you need to tell someone on your Safety Team, and keep telling until someone listens to you.

- Why do you think Gary wanted to talk to Miss Martin?
- Who are some people you could talk to if you didn't feel safe? (People on your Safety Team).

ADDITIONAL INFORMATION

Below is an introduction to some of the core concepts of the *Safe4Kids Protective Education Program*. It is important children have an understanding of these concepts to help keep them safe.

FEELINGS: When children are asked to name feelings or talk about their feelings, they find it difficult because they are not familiar with those words. Children need to understand that all feelings are okay; it's the negative behaviours that go with some feelings that are not acceptable. Everybody's feelings are different, and nobody can tell you how you should feel. Be mindful of saying to children, "Don't be scared," or "Don't be silly," when they show signs of distress or discomfort about something. Instead, brainstorm with children what they can do to make themselves feel safer if they are feeling a negative emotion.

EARLY WARNING SIGNS: Early Warning Signs are our body's way of telling us that we feel unsafe. They are our "fight, flight, or freeze" response. They are also known as our intuition or "gut feelings". Early Warning Signs can be different for each of us, and include sweaty palms, feeling unable to move, rapid heartbeat, butterflies in our tummy, goose bumps, hair standing up on our arms, etc.

SAFETY TEAM OR NETWORK: A Safety Team is five trusted adults a child can talk with if they feel unsafe. Children need to know that these trusted adults will:

- listen to them
- believe them
- be available to them and
- take action if necessary, to help them feel safe again.

Help your child develop a Safety Team who will provide support and help protect them.

PERSISTENCE: When children need help, they must be taught to persist, to keep on asking for help until they receive it. If a child needs help, the first person they approach will not always listen to them or be able to help them. Children need to persist and keep telling trusted adults on their Safety Team, until their Early Warning Signs go away and they feel safe again. Persistence is of particular value in an emergency – when you need help immediately.

NAMES OF PRIVATE BODY PARTS: It is essential children are taught the correct anatomical names for their private body parts. Their private body parts are those parts covered by their bathers, and also their mouth. This is not sex education. It is merely teaching children the correct terminology, so that if they are subjected to abuse they can disclose the abuse using the correct private body-part names, which has proven very beneficial in assisting prosecutors. It is also a deterrent for perpetrators if a child is able to use the correct names for their private body parts, since it is an indication that the child may have received some form of Protective Education.

SAYING "NO": Children are taught to respect their elders, to be polite and always to obey adults. Unfortunately, this can, and does, place them in harm's way. Children are often abused by people they know and trust. Children need to be taught that if they feel unsafe or have their Early Warning Signs it is okay to say "No" to anyone, especially if someone tries to touch their private body parts. It is also okay to break the rules of politeness and expected behaviour. If there is an emergency, then it's okay to interrupt adults, to keep themselves safe or help someone else in danger.

SECRETS: Children need to know that there are two kinds of secrets:

"Good" or "Safe" secrets are only kept for a short time, and will make someone happy when the secret is revealed. For example, a surprise birthday party, where everyone but the birthday person knows about the party for days or weeks in advance.

"Bad" or "Unsafe" secrets will make a child feel anxious, concerned or uncomfortable; they may have their Early Warning Signs. They will be told they must never tell, and that the secret must be kept for a long time, maybe even a lifetime. Unsafe secrets are kept by threats, coercion, bribes, and manipulation. Other ways children can identify a Bad or Unsafe Secret is that there may only be two people who know the secret. Children need to know they should never keep Bad or Unsafe secrets, and should always tell someone on their Safety Team. Teach children they should never keep a secret about any kind of touching, even if they like the touch or the secret little special game.

For more information on child protection education and resources visit www.safe4kids.com.au

RECEIVING A DISCLOSURE: If your child discloses that they have been abused, either physically, sexually or emotionally, here are some suggestions which may help your child, and you, to feel safe:

STAY CALM: Try to put your feelings aside, as an outraged reaction will only reinforce your child's reluctance to disclose. To help you stay calm and in control, try and remember the following three things you need to tell your child:

"I'm glad you told me"

"I believe you"

"It is not your fault".

BELIEVE YOUR CHILD: Children rarely lie about abuse, but they are often discouraged from disclosing because they think no-one will believe them. It is therefore very important they know that you believe them.

OFFER REASSURANCE: Reassure your child that it is not their fault and they haven't done anything wrong; they are not to blame. You can also use phrases such as:

"You've done the right thing by telling me," or

"I'm sorry this has happened to you and we'll work this out together."

DO NOT QUESTION YOUR CHILD: Do not pressure your child to give in-depth details. They may have to repeat their story for authorities and they may find it distressing each time they have to recount the abuse.

DO NOT APPROACH THE ALLEGED PERPETRATOR: Leave this to the authorities.

MAKE NO PROMISES: Do not promise to keep this a secret. You may have to tell the authorities about what has happened.

CONTACT AUTHORITIES

The Department for Child Protection

Police Child Protection Unit

OTHER CONTACTS:

Kids Helpline 1800 55 1800 (Australia only) or

www.kidshelpline.com.au

Manufactured by Amazon.ca
Bolton, ON